If Found, Please Return To:

_____

VITAL INFORMATION

Purchase Information

Year	Make	Model
Date of Purchase	Mileage	VIN
Purchased From		
Address		
Phone	Salesman (if applicable)	

Weight, Tow & Pressure

GCVR	
GCWR	
Tongue	
Tow Capacity	
Tire Pressure	
Notes	

Tank Capacity

Fresh	
Gray	
Gray	
Black	
Propane	
Notes	

Notes

_____
_____
_____
_____

MAINTENANCE CHECKLIST

Date _____
_____
_____

- ○ Oil Change
- ○ Oil Filter
- ○ Air Filter
- ○ Fuel Filter
- ○ Fan Belts
- ○ Radiator Hose
- ○ Water Pump
- ○ Fluid Levels
- ○ Chassis
- ○ Tires
- ○ Wipers
- ○ A/C
- ○ Lights
- ○ Battery
- ○ Dump Valve
- ○ Black Tank
- ○ Gray Tank
- ○ Window Seals
- ○ Steps
- ○ Converter
- ○ Roof A/C
- ○ Propane Tank
- ○ Generator
- ○ Fresh Water Tank

- ○ Water Heater
- ○ Stove
- ○ Refrigerator
- ○ Furnace
- ○ Fire Extinguisher
- ○ Slide Seals
- ○ Frame
- ○ Locks
- ○ Latches
- ○ Trailer Brakes
- ○ Exterior Lights
- ○ Interior Lights
- ○ Tow Coupler
- ○ Breakaway Switch
- ○ _____
- ○ _____
- ○ _____
- ○ _____
- ○ _____
- ○ _____
- ○ _____
- ○ _____
- ○ _____

MAINTENANCE NOTES

MAINTENANCE CHECKLIST

Date _____

_____

_____

- ○ Oil Change
- ○ Oil Filter
- ○ Air Filter
- ○ Fuel Filter
- ○ Fan Belts
- ○ Radiator Hose
- ○ Water Pump
- ○ Fluid Levels
- ○ Chassis
- ○ Tires
- ○ Wipers
- ○ A/C
- ○ Lights
- ○ Battery
- ○ Dump Valve
- ○ Black Tank
- ○ Gray Tank
- ○ Window Seals
- ○ Steps
- ○ Converter
- ○ Roof A/C
- ○ Propane Tank
- ○ Generator
- ○ Fresh Water Tank

- ○ Water Heater
- ○ Stove
- ○ Refrigerator
- ○ Furnace
- ○ Fire Extinguisher
- ○ Slide Seals
- ○ Frame
- ○ Locks
- ○ Latches
- ○ Trailer Brakes
- ○ Exterior Lights
- ○ Interior Lights
- ○ Tow Coupler
- ○ Breakaway Switch
- ○ _____
- ○ _____
- ○ _____
- ○ _____
- ○ _____
- ○ _____
- ○ _____
- ○ _____
- ○ _____
- ○ _____

MAINTENANCE NOTES

MAINTENANCE CHECKLIST

Date _____

_____

_____

- ○ Oil Change
- ○ Oil Filter
- ○ Air Filter
- ○ Fuel Filter
- ○ Fan Belts
- ○ Radiator Hose
- ○ Water Pump
- ○ Fluid Levels
- ○ Chassis
- ○ Tires
- ○ Wipers
- ○ A/C
- ○ Lights
- ○ Battery
- ○ Dump Valve
- ○ Black Tank
- ○ Gray Tank
- ○ Window Seals
- ○ Steps
- ○ Converter
- ○ Roof A/C
- ○ Propane Tank
- ○ Generator
- ○ Fresh Water Tank
- ○ Water Heater
- ○ Stove
- ○ Refrigerator
- ○ Furnace
- ○ Fire Extinguisher
- ○ Slide Seals
- ○ Frame
- ○ Locks
- ○ Latches
- ○ Trailer Brakes
- ○ Exterior Lights
- ○ Interior Lights
- ○ Tow Coupler
- ○ Breakaway Switch
- ○ _____
- ○ _____
- ○ _____
- ○ _____
- ○ _____
- ○ _____
- ○ _____

MAINTENANCE NOTES

MAINTENANCE CHECKLIST

Date _____

_____

_____

- ○ Oil Change
- ○ Oil Filter
- ○ Air Filter
- ○ Fuel Filter
- ○ Fan Belts
- ○ Radiator Hose
- ○ Water Pump
- ○ Fluid Levels
- ○ Chassis
- ○ Tires
- ○ Wipers
- ○ A/C
- ○ Lights
- ○ Battery
- ○ Dump Valve
- ○ Black Tank
- ○ Gray Tank
- ○ Window Seals
- ○ Steps
- ○ Converter
- ○ Roof A/C
- ○ Propane Tank
- ○ Generator
- ○ Fresh Water Tank

- ○ Water Heater
- ○ Stove
- ○ Refrigerator
- ○ Furnace
- ○ Fire Extinguisher
- ○ Slide Seals
- ○ Frame
- ○ Locks
- ○ Latches
- ○ Trailer Brakes
- ○ Exterior Lights
- ○ Interior Lights
- ○ Tow Coupler
- ○ Breakaway Switch
- ○ _____
- ○ _____
- ○ _____
- ○ _____
- ○ _____
- ○ _____
- ○ _____

MAINTENANCE NOTES

MAINTENANCE CHECKLIST

Date _____

_____

_____

- ○ Oil Change
- ○ Oil Filter
- ○ Air Filter
- ○ Fuel Filter
- ○ Fan Belts
- ○ Radiator Hose
- ○ Water Pump
- ○ Fluid Levels
- ○ Chassis
- ○ Tires
- ○ Wipers
- ○ A/C
- ○ Lights
- ○ Battery
- ○ Dump Valve
- ○ Black Tank
- ○ Gray Tank
- ○ Window Seals
- ○ Steps
- ○ Converter
- ○ Roof A/C
- ○ Propane Tank
- ○ Generator
- ○ Fresh Water Tank

- ○ Water Heater
- ○ Stove
- ○ Refrigerator
- ○ Furnace
- ○ Fire Extinguisher
- ○ Slide Seals
- ○ Frame
- ○ Locks
- ○ Latches
- ○ Trailer Brakes
- ○ Exterior Lights
- ○ Interior Lights
- ○ Tow Coupler
- ○ Breakaway Switch
- ○ _____
- ○ _____
- ○ _____
- ○ _____
- ○ _____
- ○ _____
- ○ _____
- ○ _____
- ○ _____
- ○ _____

MAINTENANCE NOTES

MAINTENANCE CHECKLIST

Date _____

_____

_____

- o Oil Change
- o Oil Filter
- o Air Filter
- o Fuel Filter
- o Fan Belts
- o Radiator Hose
- o Water Pump
- o Fluid Levels
- o Chassis
- o Tires
- o Wipers
- o A/C
- o Lights
- o Battery
- o Dump Valve
- o Black Tank
- o Gray Tank
- o Window Seals
- o Steps
- o Converter
- o Roof A/C
- o Propane Tank
- o Generator
- o Fresh Water Tank

- o Water Heater
- o Stove
- o Refrigerator
- o Furnace
- o Fire Extinguisher
- o Slide Seals
- o Frame
- o Locks
- o Latches
- o Trailer Brakes
- o Exterior Lights
- o Interior Lights
- o Tow Coupler
- o Breakaway Switch
- o _____
- o _____
- o _____
- o _____
- o _____
- o _____
- o _____
- o _____
- o _____

MAINTENANCE NOTES

MAINTENANCE CHECKLIST

Date _____

_____

_____

- ○ Oil Change
- ○ Oil Filter
- ○ Air Filter
- ○ Fuel Filter
- ○ Fan Belts
- ○ Radiator Hose
- ○ Water Pump
- ○ Fluid Levels
- ○ Chassis
- ○ Tires
- ○ Wipers
- ○ A/C
- ○ Lights
- ○ Battery
- ○ Dump Valve
- ○ Black Tank
- ○ Gray Tank
- ○ Window Seals
- ○ Steps
- ○ Converter
- ○ Roof A/C
- ○ Propane Tank
- ○ Generator
- ○ Fresh Water Tank

- ○ Water Heater
- ○ Stove
- ○ Refrigerator
- ○ Furnace
- ○ Fire Extinguisher
- ○ Slide Seals
- ○ Frame
- ○ Locks
- ○ Latches
- ○ Trailer Brakes
- ○ Exterior Lights
- ○ Interior Lights
- ○ Tow Coupler
- ○ Breakaway Switch
- ○ _____
- ○ _____
- ○ _____
- ○ _____
- ○ _____
- ○ _____
- ○ _____
- ○ _____
- ○ _____
- ○ _____

MAINTENANCE NOTES

MAINTENANCE CHECKLIST

Date _____

_____

_____

- o Oil Change
- o Oil Filter
- o Air Filter
- o Fuel Filter
- o Fan Belts
- o Radiator Hose
- o Water Pump
- o Fluid Levels
- o Chassis
- o Tires
- o Wipers
- o A/C
- o Lights
- o Battery
- o Dump Valve
- o Black Tank
- o Gray Tank
- o Window Seals
- o Steps
- o Converter
- o Roof A/C
- o Propane Tank
- o Generator
- o Fresh Water Tank

- o Water Heater
- o Stove
- o Refrigerator
- o Furnace
- o Fire Extinguisher
- o Slide Seals
- o Frame
- o Locks
- o Latches
- o Trailer Brakes
- o Exterior Lights
- o Interior Lights
- o Tow Coupler
- o Breakaway Switch
- o _____
- o _____
- o _____
- o _____
- o _____
- o _____
- o _____
- o _____

MAINTENANCE NOTES

MAINTENANCE CHECKLIST

Date _____

_____

_____

- ○ Oil Change
- ○ Oil Filter
- ○ Air Filter
- ○ Fuel Filter
- ○ Fan Belts
- ○ Radiator Hose
- ○ Water Pump
- ○ Fluid Levels
- ○ Chassis
- ○ Tires
- ○ Wipers
- ○ A/C
- ○ Lights
- ○ Battery
- ○ Dump Valve
- ○ Black Tank
- ○ Gray Tank
- ○ Window Seals
- ○ Steps
- ○ Converter
- ○ Roof A/C
- ○ Propane Tank
- ○ Generator
- ○ Fresh Water Tank

- ○ Water Heater
- ○ Stove
- ○ Refrigerator
- ○ Furnace
- ○ Fire Extinguisher
- ○ Slide Seals
- ○ Frame
- ○ Locks
- ○ Latches
- ○ Trailer Brakes
- ○ Exterior Lights
- ○ Interior Lights
- ○ Tow Coupler
- ○ Breakaway Switch
- ○ _____
- ○ _____
- ○ _____
- ○ _____
- ○ _____
- ○ _____
- ○ _____

MAINTENANCE NOTES

MAINTENANCE CHECKLIST

Date _____

_____

_____

- ○ Oil Change
- ○ Oil Filter
- ○ Air Filter
- ○ Fuel Filter
- ○ Fan Belts
- ○ Radiator Hose
- ○ Water Pump
- ○ Fluid Levels
- ○ Chassis
- ○ Tires
- ○ Wipers
- ○ A/C
- ○ Lights
- ○ Battery
- ○ Dump Valve
- ○ Black Tank
- ○ Gray Tank
- ○ Window Seals
- ○ Steps
- ○ Converter
- ○ Roof A/C
- ○ Propane Tank
- ○ Generator
- ○ Fresh Water Tank

- ○ Water Heater
- ○ Stove
- ○ Refrigerator
- ○ Furnace
- ○ Fire Extinguisher
- ○ Slide Seals
- ○ Frame
- ○ Locks
- ○ Latches
- ○ Trailer Brakes
- ○ Exterior Lights
- ○ Interior Lights
- ○ Tow Coupler
- ○ Breakaway Switch
- ○ _____
- ○ _____
- ○ _____
- ○ _____
- ○ _____
- ○ _____
- ○ _____
- ○ _____

MAINTENANCE NOTES

TRIP LOG

Reservation Information

Park Name

Address

Phone   Email

Confirmation #   Reservation Co. (KOA)

Check-In   Check Out

Cancellation Policy   Cancellation Fee

50 amp   30 amp   Full HU   Water   Electric   No Util

Site #   Length   Width   Rate $

OTHER NOTES

_____
_____
_____
_____
_____
_____
_____
_____
_____
_____
_____

TRIP CHECKLIST

- Sheets
- Sleeping Bag
- Pillows
- Towels
- Wash Cloths
- Paper Towels
- Toilet Paper
- Garbage Bags
- Table Cloths
- Plastic Utensils
- Paper Plates
- Napkins
- Dish Soap
- Foil
- Plastic Wrap
- Lighter/Matches
- Batteries
- Dustpan
- Broom
- Bug Spray
- Candles
- Cell Phone Charger
- Medication
- Sunscreen
- Lip Balm

- Cooking Utensils
- Cooler
- Ice
- Rain Gear
- _____
- _____
- _____
- _____
- _____
- _____
- _____
- _____
- _____
- _____
- _____
- _____
- _____
- _____
- _____
- _____
- _____
- _____
- _____
- _____
- _____

MEAL PLANNER

	BREAKFAST	LUNCH	DINNER
DAY 1			
DAY 2			
DAY 3			
DAY 4			
DAY 5			
DAY 6			
DAY 7			

GROCERY SHOPPING LIST

TRIP MEMORIES

TRIP LOG

Reservation Information

Park Name

Address

Phone   Email

Confirmation #   Reservation Co. (KOA)

Check-In   Check Out

Cancellation Policy   Cancellation Fee

50 amp   30 amp   Full HU   Water   Electric   No Util

Site #   Length   Width   Rate $

OTHER NOTES

_____
_____
_____
_____
_____
_____
_____
_____
_____
_____
_____

TRIP CHECKLIST

- ○ Sheets
- ○ Sleeping Bag
- ○ Pillows
- ○ Towels
- ○ Wash Cloths
- ○ Paper Towels
- ○ Toilet Paper
- ○ Garbage Bags
- ○ Table Cloths
- ○ Plastic Utensils
- ○ Paper Plates
- ○ Napkins
- ○ Dish Soap
- ○ Foil
- ○ Plastic Wrap
- ○ Lighter/Matches
- ○ Batteries
- ○ Dustpan
- ○ Broom
- ○ Bug Spray
- ○ Candles
- ○ Cell Phone Charger
- ○ Medication
- ○ Sunscreen
- ○ Lip Balm

- ○ Cooking Utensils
- ○ Cooler
- ○ Ice
- ○ Rain Gear
- ○ _____
- ○ _____
- ○ _____
- ○ _____
- ○ _____
- ○ _____
- ○ _____
- ○ _____
- ○ _____
- ○ _____
- ○ _____
- ○ _____
- ○ _____
- ○ _____
- ○ _____
- ○ _____
- ○ _____
- ○ _____
- ○ _____
- ○ _____
- ○ _____

MEAL PLANNER

	BREAKFAST	LUNCH	DINNER
DAY 1			
DAY 2			
DAY 3			
DAY 4			
DAY 5			
DAY 6			
DAY 7			

GROCERY SHOPPING LIST

TRIP MEMORIES

TRIP PHOTOS

TRIP LOG

Reservation Information

Park Name

Address

Phone   Email

Confirmation #   Reservation Co. (KOA)

Check-In   Check Out

Cancellation Policy   Cancellation Fee

50 amp   30 amp   Full HU   Water   Electric   No Util

Site #   Length   Width   Rate $

OTHER NOTES

_____
_____
_____
_____
_____
_____
_____
_____
_____
_____
_____

TRIP CHECKLIST

- ☐ Sheets
- ☐ Sleeping Bag
- ☐ Pillows
- ☐ Towels
- ☐ Wash Cloths
- ☐ Paper Towels
- ☐ Toilet Paper
- ☐ Garbage Bags
- ☐ Table Cloths
- ☐ Plastic Utensils
- ☐ Paper Plates
- ☐ Napkins
- ☐ Dish Soap
- ☐ Foil
- ☐ Plastic Wrap
- ☐ Lighter/Matches
- ☐ Batteries
- ☐ Dustpan
- ☐ Broom
- ☐ Bug Spray
- ☐ Candles
- ☐ Cell Phone Charger
- ☐ Medication
- ☐ Sunscreen
- ☐ Lip Balm

- ☐ Cooking Utensils
- ☐ Cooler
- ☐ Ice
- ☐ Rain Gear
- ☐ _____
- ☐ _____
- ☐ _____
- ☐ _____
- ☐ _____
- ☐ _____
- ☐ _____
- ☐ _____
- ☐ _____
- ☐ _____
- ☐ _____
- ☐ _____
- ☐ _____
- ☐ _____
- ☐ _____
- ☐ _____
- ☐ _____
- ☐ _____
- ☐ _____
- ☐ _____
- ☐ _____

MEAL PLANNER

	BREAKFAST	LUNCH	DINNER
DAY 1			
DAY 2			
DAY 3			
DAY 4			
DAY 5			
DAY 6			
DAY 7			

GROCERY SHOPPING LIST

TRIP MEMORIES

TRIP PHOTOS

TRIP LOG

Reservation Information

Park Name

Address

Phone   Email

Confirmation #   Reservation Co. (KOA)

Check-In   Check Out

Cancellation Policy   Cancellation Fee

50 amp   30 amp   Full HU   Water   Electric   No Util

Site #   Length   Width   Rate $

OTHER NOTES

_____
_____
_____
_____
_____
_____
_____
_____
_____
_____
_____

TRIP CHECKLIST

- ○ Sheets
- ○ Sleeping Bag
- ○ Pillows
- ○ Towels
- ○ Wash Cloths
- ○ Paper Towels
- ○ Toilet Paper
- ○ Garbage Bags
- ○ Table Cloths
- ○ Plastic Utensils
- ○ Paper Plates
- ○ Napkins
- ○ Dish Soap
- ○ Foil
- ○ Plastic Wrap
- ○ Lighter/Matches
- ○ Batteries
- ○ Dustpan
- ○ Broom
- ○ Bug Spray
- ○ Candles
- ○ Cell Phone Charger
- ○ Medication
- ○ Sunscreen
- ○ Lip Balm

- ○ Cooking Utensils
- ○ Cooler
- ○ Ice
- ○ Rain Gear
- ○ _____
- ○ _____
- ○ _____
- ○ _____
- ○ _____
- ○ _____
- ○ _____
- ○ _____
- ○ _____
- ○ _____
- ○ _____
- ○ _____
- ○ _____
- ○ _____
- ○ _____
- ○ _____
- ○ _____
- ○ _____
- ○ _____
- ○ _____
- ○ _____

MEAL PLANNER

	BREAKFAST	LUNCH	DINNER
DAY 1			
DAY 2			
DAY 3			
DAY 4			
DAY 5			
DAY 6			
DAY 7			

GROCERY SHOPPING LIST

TRIP MEMORIES

TRIP PHOTOS

TRIP LOG

Reservation Information

Park Name

Address

Phone   Email

Confirmation #   Reservation Co. (KOA)

Check-In   Check Out

Cancellation Policy   Cancellation Fee

50 amp   30 amp   Full HU   Water   Electric   No Util

Site #   Length   Width   Rate $

OTHER NOTES

_____
_____
_____
_____
_____
_____
_____
_____
_____
_____
_____

TRIP CHECKLIST

- Sheets
- Sleeping Bag
- Pillows
- Towels
- Wash Cloths
- Paper Towels
- Toilet Paper
- Garbage Bags
- Table Cloths
- Plastic Utensils
- Paper Plates
- Napkins
- Dish Soap
- Foil
- Plastic Wrap
- Lighter/Matches
- Batteries
- Dustpan
- Broom
- Bug Spray
- Candles
- Cell Phone Charger
- Medication
- Sunscreen
- Lip Balm

- Cooking Utensils
- Cooler
- Ice
- Rain Gear
- _____
- _____
- _____
- _____
- _____
- _____
- _____
- _____
- _____
- _____
- _____
- _____
- _____
- _____
- _____
- _____
- _____
- _____
- _____
- _____
- _____

MEAL PLANNER

	BREAKFAST	LUNCH	DINNER
DAY 1			
DAY 2			
DAY 3			
DAY 4			
DAY 5			
DAY 6			
DAY 7			

GROCERY SHOPPING LIST

TRIP MEMORIES

TRIP PHOTOS

TRIP LOG

Reservation Information

Park Name

Address

Phone   Email

Confirmation #   Reservation Co. (KOA)

Check-In   Check Out

Cancellation Policy   Cancellation Fee

50 amp   30 amp   Full HU   Water   Electric   No Util

Site #   Length   Width   Rate $

OTHER NOTES

_____
_____
_____
_____
_____
_____
_____
_____
_____
_____

TRIP CHECKLIST

- ○ Sheets
- ○ Sleeping Bag
- ○ Pillows
- ○ Towels
- ○ Wash Cloths
- ○ Paper Towels
- ○ Toilet Paper
- ○ Garbage Bags
- ○ Table Cloths
- ○ Plastic Utensils
- ○ Paper Plates
- ○ Napkins
- ○ Dish Soap
- ○ Foil
- ○ Plastic Wrap
- ○ Lighter/Matches
- ○ Batteries
- ○ Dustpan
- ○ Broom
- ○ Bug Spray
- ○ Candles
- ○ Cell Phone Charger
- ○ Medication
- ○ Sunscreen
- ○ Lip Balm

- ○ Cooking Utensils
- ○ Cooler
- ○ Ice
- ○ Rain Gear
- ○ _____
- ○ _____
- ○ _____
- ○ _____
- ○ _____
- ○ _____
- ○ _____
- ○ _____
- ○ _____
- ○ _____
- ○ _____
- ○ _____
- ○ _____
- ○ _____
- ○ _____
- ○ _____
- ○ _____
- ○ _____
- ○ _____
- ○ _____
- ○ _____

MEAL PLANNER

	BREAKFAST	LUNCH	DINNER
DAY 1			
DAY 2			
DAY 3			
DAY 4			
DAY 5			
DAY 6			
DAY 7			

GROCERY SHOPPING LIST

TRIP MEMORIES

TRIP PHOTOS

TRIP LOG

Reservation Information

Park Name

Address

Phone   Email

Confirmation #   Reservation Co. (KOA)

Check-In   Check Out

Cancellation Policy   Cancellation Fee

50 amp   30 amp   Full HU   Water   Electric   No Util

Site #   Length   Width   Rate $

OTHER NOTES

_____
_____
_____
_____
_____
_____
_____
_____
_____
_____
_____

TRIP CHECKLIST

- ☐ Sheets
- ☐ Sleeping Bag
- ☐ Pillows
- ☐ Towels
- ☐ Wash Cloths
- ☐ Paper Towels
- ☐ Toilet Paper
- ☐ Garbage Bags
- ☐ Table Cloths
- ☐ Plastic Utensils
- ☐ Paper Plates
- ☐ Napkins
- ☐ Dish Soap
- ☐ Foil
- ☐ Plastic Wrap
- ☐ Lighter/Matches
- ☐ Batteries
- ☐ Dustpan
- ☐ Broom
- ☐ Bug Spray
- ☐ Candles
- ☐ Cell Phone Charger
- ☐ Medication
- ☐ Sunscreen
- ☐ Lip Balm

- ☐ Cooking Utensils
- ☐ Cooler
- ☐ Ice
- ☐ Rain Gear
- ☐ _____
- ☐ _____
- ☐ _____
- ☐ _____
- ☐ _____
- ☐ _____
- ☐ _____
- ☐ _____
- ☐ _____
- ☐ _____
- ☐ _____
- ☐ _____
- ☐ _____
- ☐ _____
- ☐ _____
- ☐ _____
- ☐ _____
- ☐ _____
- ☐ _____
- ☐ _____

MEAL PLANNER

	BREAKFAST	LUNCH	DINNER
DAY 1			
DAY 2			
DAY 3			
DAY 4			
DAY 5			
DAY 6			
DAY 7			

GROCERY SHOPPING LIST

TRIP MEMORIES

TRIP PHOTOS

TRIP LOG

Reservation Information

Park Name

Address

Phone   Email

Confirmation #   Reservation Co. (KOA)

Check-In   Check Out

Cancellation Policy   Cancellation Fee

50 amp   30 amp   Full HU   Water   Electric   No Util

Site #   Length   Width   Rate $

OTHER NOTES

_____
_____
_____
_____
_____
_____
_____
_____
_____
_____

TRIP CHECKLIST

- Sheets
- Sleeping Bag
- Pillows
- Towels
- Wash Cloths
- Paper Towels
- Toilet Paper
- Garbage Bags
- Table Cloths
- Plastic Utensils
- Paper Plates
- Napkins
- Dish Soap
- Foil
- Plastic Wrap
- Lighter/Matches
- Batteries
- Dustpan
- Broom
- Bug Spray
- Candles
- Cell Phone Charger
- Medication
- Sunscreen
- Lip Balm

- Cooking Utensils
- Cooler
- Ice
- Rain Gear
- _____
- _____
- _____
- _____
- _____
- _____
- _____
- _____
- _____
- _____
- _____
- _____
- _____
- _____
- _____
- _____
- _____
- _____
- _____
- _____
- _____

MEAL PLANNER

	BREAKFAST	LUNCH	DINNER
DAY 1			
DAY 2			
DAY 3			
DAY 4			
DAY 5			
DAY 6			
DAY 7			

GROCERY SHOPPING LIST

TRIP MEMORIES

TRIP PHOTOS

TRIP LOG

Reservation Information

Park Name

Address

Phone   Email

Confirmation #   Reservation Co. (KOA)

Check-In   Check Out

Cancellation Policy   Cancellation Fee

50 amp   30 amp   Full HU   Water   Electric   No Util

Site #   Length   Width   Rate $

OTHER NOTES

_____
_____
_____
_____
_____
_____
_____
_____
_____
_____
_____

TRIP CHECKLIST

- ○ Sheets
- ○ Sleeping Bag
- ○ Pillows
- ○ Towels
- ○ Wash Cloths
- ○ Paper Towels
- ○ Toilet Paper
- ○ Garbage Bags
- ○ Table Cloths
- ○ Plastic Utensils
- ○ Paper Plates
- ○ Napkins
- ○ Dish Soap
- ○ Foil
- ○ Plastic Wrap
- ○ Lighter/Matches
- ○ Batteries
- ○ Dustpan
- ○ Broom
- ○ Bug Spray
- ○ Candles
- ○ Cell Phone Charger
- ○ Medication
- ○ Sunscreen
- ○ Lip Balm

- ○ Cooking Utensils
- ○ Cooler
- ○ Ice
- ○ Rain Gear
- ○ _____
- ○ _____
- ○ _____
- ○ _____
- ○ _____
- ○ _____
- ○ _____
- ○ _____
- ○ _____
- ○ _____
- ○ _____
- ○ _____
- ○ _____
- ○ _____
- ○ _____
- ○ _____
- ○ _____
- ○ _____
- ○ _____

MEAL PLANNER

	BREAKFAST	LUNCH	DINNER
DAY 1			
DAY 2			
DAY 3			
DAY 4			
DAY 5			
DAY 6			
DAY 7			

GROCERY SHOPPING LIST

TRIP MEMORIES

TRIP PHOTOS

TRIP LOG

Reservation Information

Park Name

Address

Phone   Email

Confirmation #   Reservation Co. (KOA)

Check-In   Check Out

Cancellation Policy   Cancellation Fee

50 amp   30 amp   Full HU   Water   Electric   No Util

Site #   Length   Width   Rate $

OTHER NOTES

_____
_____
_____
_____
_____
_____
_____
_____
_____
_____
_____

TRIP CHECKLIST

- ○ Sheets
- ○ Sleeping Bag
- ○ Pillows
- ○ Towels
- ○ Wash Cloths
- ○ Paper Towels
- ○ Toilet Paper
- ○ Garbage Bags
- ○ Table Cloths
- ○ Plastic Utensils
- ○ Paper Plates
- ○ Napkins
- ○ Dish Soap
- ○ Foil
- ○ Plastic Wrap
- ○ Lighter/Matches
- ○ Batteries
- ○ Dustpan
- ○ Broom
- ○ Bug Spray
- ○ Candles
- ○ Cell Phone Charger
- ○ Medication
- ○ Sunscreen
- ○ Lip Balm

- ○ Cooking Utensils
- ○ Cooler
- ○ Ice
- ○ Rain Gear
- ○ _____
- ○ _____
- ○ _____
- ○ _____
- ○ _____
- ○ _____
- ○ _____
- ○ _____
- ○ _____
- ○ _____
- ○ _____
- ○ _____
- ○ _____
- ○ _____
- ○ _____
- ○ _____
- ○ _____
- ○ _____
- ○ _____
- ○ _____
- ○ _____

MEAL PLANNER

	BREAKFAST	LUNCH	DINNER
DAY 1			
DAY 2			
DAY 3			
DAY 4			
DAY 5			
DAY 6			
DAY 7			

GROCERY SHOPPING LIST

TRIP MEMORIES

TRIP PHOTOS

TRIP LOG

Reservation Information

Park Name

Address

Phone   Email

Confirmation #   Reservation Co. (KOA)

Check-In   Check Out

Cancellation Policy   Cancellation Fee

50 amp   30 amp   Full HU   Water   Electric   No Util

Site #   Length   Width   Rate $

OTHER NOTES

_____
_____
_____
_____
_____
_____
_____
_____
_____
_____

TRIP CHECKLIST

- ○ Sheets
- ○ Sleeping Bag
- ○ Pillows
- ○ Towels
- ○ Wash Cloths
- ○ Paper Towels
- ○ Toilet Paper
- ○ Garbage Bags
- ○ Table Cloths
- ○ Plastic Utensils
- ○ Paper Plates
- ○ Napkins
- ○ Dish Soap
- ○ Foil
- ○ Plastic Wrap
- ○ Lighter/Matches
- ○ Batteries
- ○ Dustpan
- ○ Broom
- ○ Bug Spray
- ○ Candles
- ○ Cell Phone Charger
- ○ Medication
- ○ Sunscreen
- ○ Lip Balm

- ○ Cooking Utensils
- ○ Cooler
- ○ Ice
- ○ Rain Gear
- ○ _____
- ○ _____
- ○ _____
- ○ _____
- ○ _____
- ○ _____
- ○ _____
- ○ _____
- ○ _____
- ○ _____
- ○ _____
- ○ _____
- ○ _____
- ○ _____
- ○ _____
- ○ _____
- ○ _____
- ○ _____
- ○ _____
- ○ _____

MEAL PLANNER

	BREAKFAST	LUNCH	DINNER
DAY 1			
DAY 2			
DAY 3			
DAY 4			
DAY 5			
DAY 6			
DAY 7			

GROCERY SHOPPING LIST

TRIP MEMORIES

TRIP PHOTOS

TRIP LOG

Reservation Information

Park Name

Address

Phone   Email

Confirmation #   Reservation Co. (KOA)

Check-In   Check Out

Cancellation Policy   Cancellation Fee

50 amp   30 amp   Full HU   Water   Electric   No Util

Site #   Length   Width   Rate $

OTHER NOTES

_____
_____
_____
_____
_____
_____
_____
_____
_____
_____

TRIP CHECKLIST

- ○ Sheets
- ○ Sleeping Bag
- ○ Pillows
- ○ Towels
- ○ Wash Cloths
- ○ Paper Towels
- ○ Toilet Paper
- ○ Garbage Bags
- ○ Table Cloths
- ○ Plastic Utensils
- ○ Paper Plates
- ○ Napkins
- ○ Dish Soap
- ○ Foil
- ○ Plastic Wrap
- ○ Lighter/Matches
- ○ Batteries
- ○ Dustpan
- ○ Broom
- ○ Bug Spray
- ○ Candles
- ○ Cell Phone Charger
- ○ Medication
- ○ Sunscreen
- ○ Lip Balm

- ○ Cooking Utensils
- ○ Cooler
- ○ Ice
- ○ Rain Gear
- ○ _____
- ○ _____
- ○ _____
- ○ _____
- ○ _____
- ○ _____
- ○ _____
- ○ _____
- ○ _____
- ○ _____
- ○ _____
- ○ _____
- ○ _____
- ○ _____
- ○ _____
- ○ _____
- ○ _____
- ○ _____
- ○ _____
- ○ _____

MEAL PLANNER

	BREAKFAST	LUNCH	DINNER
DAY 1			
DAY 2			
DAY 3			
DAY 4			
DAY 5			
DAY 6			
DAY 7			

GROCERY SHOPPING LIST

TRIP MEMORIES

TRIP PHOTOS

Habit Tracker

Month _____

Year _____

Day										
1										
2										
3										
4										
5										
6										
7										
8										
9										
10										
11										
12										
13										
14										
15										
16										
17										
18										
19										
20										
21										
22										
23										
24										
25										
26										
27										
28										
29										
30										
31										

Habit Tracker

Month _____

Year _____

Day												
1												
2												
3												
4												
5												
6												
7												
8												
9												
10												
11												
12												
13												
14												
15												
16												
17												
18												
19												
20												
21												
22												
23												
24												
25												
26												
27												
28												
29												
30												
31												

Habit Tracker

Month _____

Year _____

Day

1											
2											
3											
4											
5											
6											
7											
8											
9											
10											
11											
12											
13											
14											
15											
16											
17											
18											
19											
20											
21											
22											
23											
24											
25											
26											
27											
28											
29											
30											
31											

Habit Tracker

Month _____

Year _____

Day												
1												
2												
3												
4												
5												
6												
7												
8												
9												
10												
11												
12												
13												
14												
15												
16												
17												
18												
19												
20												
21												
22												
23												
24												
25												
26												
27												
28												
29												
30												
31												

Habit Tracker

Month _____

Year _____

Day												
1												
2												
3												
4												
5												
6												
7												
8												
9												
10												
11												
12												
13												
14												
15												
16												
17												
18												
19												
20												
21												
22												
23												
24												
25												
26												
27												
28												
29												
30												
31												

Habit Tracker

Month _____
Year _____

Day											
1											
2											
3											
4											
5											
6											
7											
8											
9											
10											
11											
12											
13											
14											
15											
16											
17											
18											
19											
20											
21											
22											
23											
24											
25											
26											
27											
28											
29											
30											
31											

Habit Tracker

Month _____

Year _____

Day											
1											
2											
3											
4											
5											
6											
7											
8											
9											
10											
11											
12											
13											
14											
15											
16											
17											
18											
19											
20											
21											
22											
23											
24											
25											
26											
27											
28											
29											
30											
31											

Habit Tracker

Month _____

Year _____

Day													
1													
2													
3													
4													
5													
6													
7													
8													
9													
10													
11													
12													
13													
14													
15													
16													
17													
18													
19													
20													
21													
22													
23													
24													
25													
26													
27													
28													
29													
30													
31													

Habit Tracker

Month _____

Year _____

Day

1														
2														
3														
4														
5														
6														
7														
8														
9														
10														
11														
12														
13														
14														
15														
16														
17														
18														
19														
20														
21														
22														
23														
24														
25														
26														
27														
28														
29														
30														
31														

Habit Tracker

Month _____

Year _____

Day

Habit Tracker

Month _____

Year _____

Day											
1											
2											
3											
4											
5											
6											
7											
8											
9											
10											
11											
12											
13											
14											
15											
16											
17											
18											
19											
20											
21											
22											
23											
24											
25											
26											
27											
28											
29											
30											
31											

Habit Tracker

Month _____

Year _____

Day												
1												
2												
3												
4												
5												
6												
7												
8												
9												
10												
11												
12												
13												
14												
15												
16												
17												
18												
19												
20												
21												
22												
23												
24												
25												
26												
27												
28												
29												
30												
31												

Habit Tracker

Month _____

Year _____

Day											
1											
2											
3											
4											
5											
6											
7											
8											
9											
10											
11											
12											
13											
14											
15											
16											
17											
18											
19											
20											
21											
22											
23											
24											
25											
26											
27											
28											
29											
30											
31											

Habit Tracker

Month _____

Year _____

Day											
1											
2											
3											
4											
5											
6											
7											
8											
9											
10											
11											
12											
13											
14											
15											
16											
17											
18											
19											
20											
21											
22											
23											
24											
25											
26											
27											
28											
29											
30											
31											

Habit Tracker

Month _____

Year _____

Day

1											
2											
3											
4											
5											
6											
7											
8											
9											
10											
11											
12											
13											
14											
15											
16											
17											
18											
19											
20											
21											
22											
23											
24											
25											
26											
27											
28											
29											
30											
31											

Habit Tracker

Month _____

Year _____

Day												
1												
2												
3												
4												
5												
6												
7												
8												
9												
10												
11												
12												
13												
14												
15												
16												
17												
18												
19												
20												
21												
22												
23												
24												
25												
26												
27												
28												
29												
30												
31												

Habit Tracker

Month _____

Year _____

Day											
1											
2											
3											
4											
5											
6											
7											
8											
9											
10											
11											
12											
13											
14											
15											
16											
17											
18											
19											
20											
21											
22											
23											
24											
25											
26											
27											
28											
29											
30											
31											

Habit Tracker

Month _____
Year _____

Day											
1											
2											
3											
4											
5											
6											
7											
8											
9											
10											
11											
12											
13											
14											
15											
16											
17											
18											
19											
20											
21											
22											
23											
24											
25											
26											
27											
28											
29											
30											
31											

Habit Tracker

Month _____

Year _____

Day											
1											
2											
3											
4											
5											
6											
7											
8											
9											
10											
11											
12											
13											
14											
15											
16											
17											
18											
19											
20											
21											
22											
23											
24											
25											
26											
27											
28											
29											
30											
31											

Habit Tracker

Month _____

Year _____

Day											
1											
2											
3											
4											
5											
6											
7											
8											
9											
10											
11											
12											
13											
14											
15											
16											
17											
18											
19											
20											
21											
22											
23											
24											
25											
26											
27											
28											
29											
30											
31											

Habit Tracker

Month _____

Year _____

Day															
1															
2															
3															
4															
5															
6															
7															
8															
9															
10															
11															
12															
13															
14															
15															
16															
17															
18															
19															
20															
21															
22															
23															
24															
25															
26															
27															
28															
29															
30															
31															

Habit Tracker Month _____
Year _____

Day

1											
2											
3											
4											
5											
6											
7											
8											
9											
10											
11											
12											
13											
14											
15											
16											
17											
18											
19											
20											
21											
22											
23											
24											
25											
26											
27											
28											
29											
30											
31											

Habit Tracker

Month _____

Year _____

Day												
1												
2												
3												
4												
5												
6												
7												
8												
9												
10												
11												
12												
13												
14												
15												
16												
17												
18												
19												
20												
21												
22												
23												
24												
25												
26												
27												
28												
29												
30												
31												

Habit Tracker

Month _____

Year _____

Day											
1											
2											
3											
4											
5											
6											
7											
8											
9											
10											
11											
12											
13											
14											
15											
16											
17											
18											
19											
20											
21											
22											
23											
24											
25											
26											
27											
28											
29											
30											
31											

Habit Tracker

Month _____

Year _____

Day												
1												
2												
3												
4												
5												
6												
7												
8												
9												
10												
11												
12												
13												
14												
15												
16												
17												
18												
19												
20												
21												
22												
23												
24												
25												
26												
27												
28												
29												
30												
31												

Habit Tracker   Month _____   Year _____

Day												
1												
2												
3												
4												
5												
6												
7												
8												
9												
10												
11												
12												
13												
14												
15												
16												
17												
18												
19												
20												
21												
22												
23												
24												
25												
26												
27												
28												
29												
30												
31												

www.ingramcontent.com/pod-product-compliance
Lightning Source LLC
LaVergne TN
LVHW012117070526
838202LV00056B/5752